Smart Money Skills for Teens: An Interactive Adventure in Budgeting and Credit

Kristen Roberts

Illustrated by

Ed Simkins

Copyright © 2025 by Kristen Roberts.
All rights reserved. No part of this publication may be reproduced, distributed, or transmitted in any form or by any means, including photocopying, recording, or other electronic or mechanical methods, without the prior written permission of the publisher, except in the case of brief quotations embodied in critical reviews and certain other noncommercial uses permitted by copyright law.
For inquiries, contact the publisher at KrisRAuthor@gmail.com.

Publisher's Note: This is a work of fiction. Names, characters, places, and incidents are a product of the author's imagination. Locales and public names are sometimes used for atmospheric purposes. Any resemblance to actual people, living or dead, or to businesses, companies, events, institutions, or locales is completely coincidental.
Chicago – First Edition
ISBN 979-8-9917246-3-0
Printed in the United States of America

Mom, thanks for always encouraging me. This is for you.

CONTENTS

Introduction 1

The Paths You Can Take 3

Coffee, Cereal, and Credit 5

Commencing Credit 11

Financial Foundations 13

A Walk to Wisdom 15

Scoring Points 19

Game On! 23

Damage Control 25

Diamond Disaster 27

Tech Temptation 29

Financial Flashback 33

Scoops and Savings 35

A Cushion for Crisis 39

Concert Conundrum 43

Fun and Funds 45

Path to Prosperity 49

The Impulse Purchase 53

Debt Dilemma 55

Conversations and Choices 59

Budgeting Basics 61

The Silent Struggle 67

Denied and Distraught 69

End of our Adventure 75

Test Your Knowledge 77

Did you know? 83

Glossary 85

Notes 91

INTRODUCTION

Welcome to *Smart Money Skills for Teens: An Interactive Adventure in Budgeting & Credit!* Join Max and Jamie as they set off on an exciting journey to master the essentials of credit cards and money management, which will help *you* out in real life! Whether you're just learning about how to handle money, or you already know a bit about it, this adventure is designed to help you on your path to a fantastic financial future.

Have you been eyeing some cool new beauty products, or that latest video game console, wondering how you could afford it? Maybe you're starting to think about how to manage your college spending money? If so, this book is your secret weapon! As you explore the lives of Max and Jamie, you'll learn the tricks to saving up and making smart choices that could help turn your goals into reality.

Now for our story...

Max and Jamie are teenagers and best friends from Maplewood, coming from very different financial backgrounds. Max lives with his loving grandma in a small house on the edge of town. Money is tight, there's never any extra, and Max has never really learned how to manage it himself. He spends a lot of time at Jamie's house, where he can't help but notice how Jamie's family seems to handle money so well.

Jamie lives in a spacious two-story house in the heart of Maplewood. His parents both have good jobs, and they regularly talk about things like budgeting and savings goals. Jamie loves cracking jokes and coming up with fun ways to explain things, especially to his younger sister, Lily.

Despite their differences, Max and Jamie are inseparable. They do everything together, from playing video games to working at Sundae Sanctuary, the local ice cream shop. They'll even be going to the same university in the fall.

In this adventure, it's up to you to help Max and Jamie navigate their financial decisions. Every choice you make for them will result in different outcomes, just like how every decision you make for yourself influences your future! Will you guide them to save for college, or will you unknowingly damage their credit score? The outcome is entirely up to you!

And if you're up for a challenge, flip to the "Test Your Knowledge" section on page 77 after each chapter to see how much you've learned!

Oh, and if you see any words in **bold** later on, you can find their meanings in the Glossary at the end of the book.

THE PATHS YOU CAN TAKE

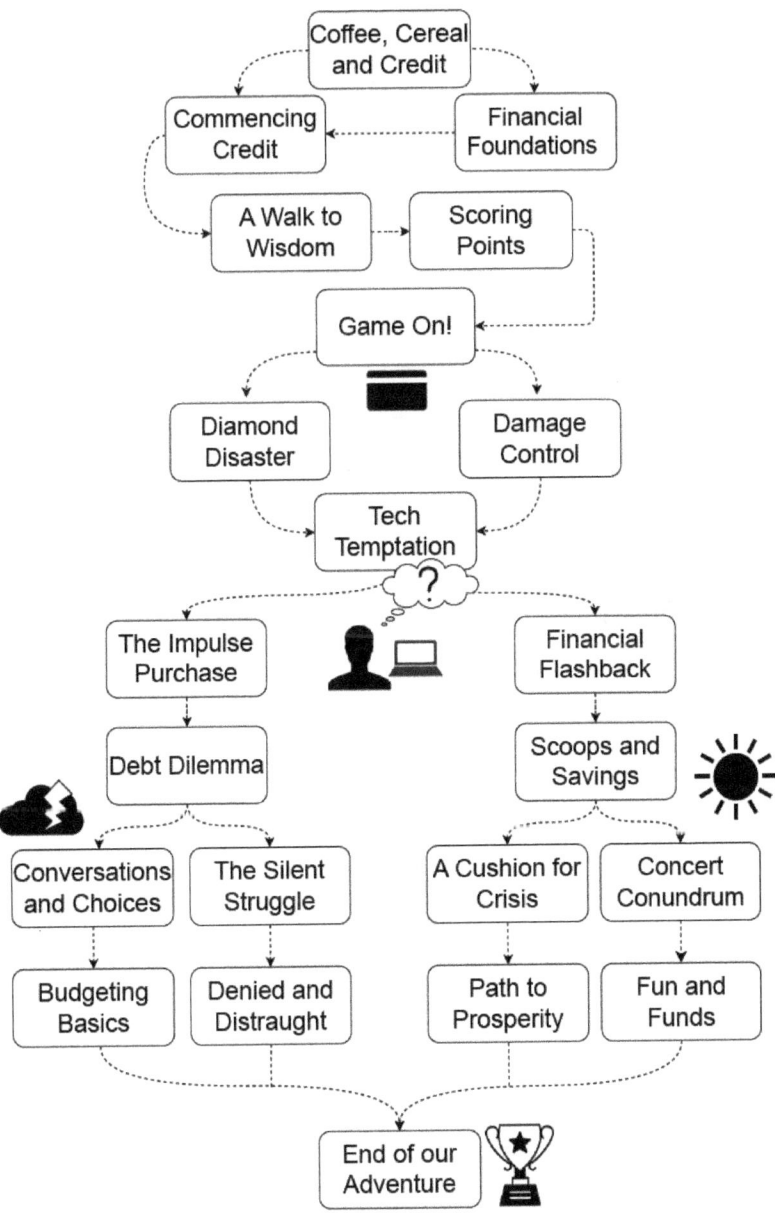

COFFEE, CEREAL, AND CREDIT

The Saturday morning sunlight streams through the kitchen window, lighting up the table where Jamie pokes absentmindedly at his pancakes. Lily is on a mission to snag the last one, her nine-year-old determination (and appetite!) on full display as she glares at her dad, who's reaching for it too.

"Dad! That's mine!" she declares, practically diving across the table with her fork.

Dad laughs, retreating with his hands up. "Alright, alright! It's all yours, kiddo."

Jamie stares at his dad's coffee mug, his fork now hovering over his plate. His stomach churns at the thought of what he's about to say to his parents. He's been thinking about this for weeks and it was time to find out if they thought he was ready.

He sets the fork down, shuts his eyes briefly, and says, "Mom, Dad...I've been thinking... and I'd like to get a **credit card**."

The table goes quiet for a beat. Dad raises an eyebrow, while Mom sets down a bowl of blueberries, a warm smile reaching her eyes.

"Really?" she asks, sitting down and folding her hands. "What brought this on?"

Jamie shrugs, leaning back in his chair. His foot taps under the table, giving him away. "I mean, I just turned 18, so I can actually get one now. Plus, with college coming up, it seems like a good time to figure out how to handle money."

Dad takes a sip of his coffee, raising an eyebrow. "A credit card, huh? That's a big move. Think you're ready for it?"

Jamie nods. "Yeah. It's not like I'm going to go crazy with it or anything."

Across the table, Lily has shifted her attention to her cereal. She looks up, milk dripping off her spoon. "Can I get a credit card too? I'd buy a whole store of candy. Wait... what even *is* a credit card? Is it like... free money?"

Jamie can't help but laugh, grateful for the distraction. "I wish it were free money!" He leans forward, waving his fork at her. "It's more like *borrowing* money from the bank to buy stuff."

Lily scrunches her nose. "So, it's like... using your library card to borrow books? You use your credit card to borrow money?"

"Right!" Jamie says, nodding toward the pile of Lily's library books on the counter.

Coffee, Cereal, and Credit

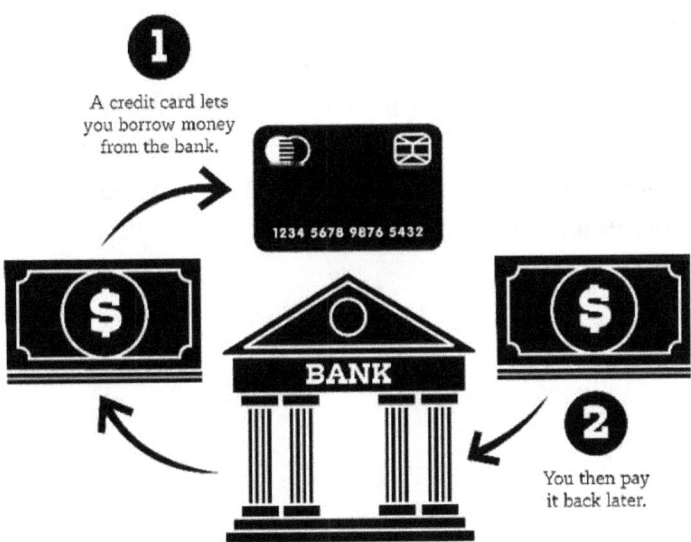

"Ooh!" Lily says. "I get it!" She grins, swinging her legs under the table.

Dad looks at Jamie, raising his mug in approval. "It's good you're thinking about this now. Credit cards can be useful, but you've got to keep track of your spending to avoid…"

"**Interest**," Jamie interrupts, a small grin spreading across his face.

Dad nods, smiling. "Exactly."

Lily, mid-bite of cereal, looks up with her cheeks puffed out like a chipmunk. "What's interest?"

Jamie taps his fork against the table as he thinks. "Alright, Lil, let's make it simple. Let's pretend you let your friend PJ borrow your chess set."

"She loves chess!" Lily blurts out, nearly spitting out cereal in excitement.

Jamie laughs. "So, PJ says she'll give it back to you on Friday, right? She also agrees to give you a sticker for each day that she keeps it longer than that. So, if she forgets and keeps the chess set longer—say, until Monday— then she owes you three stickers when she finally gives it back."

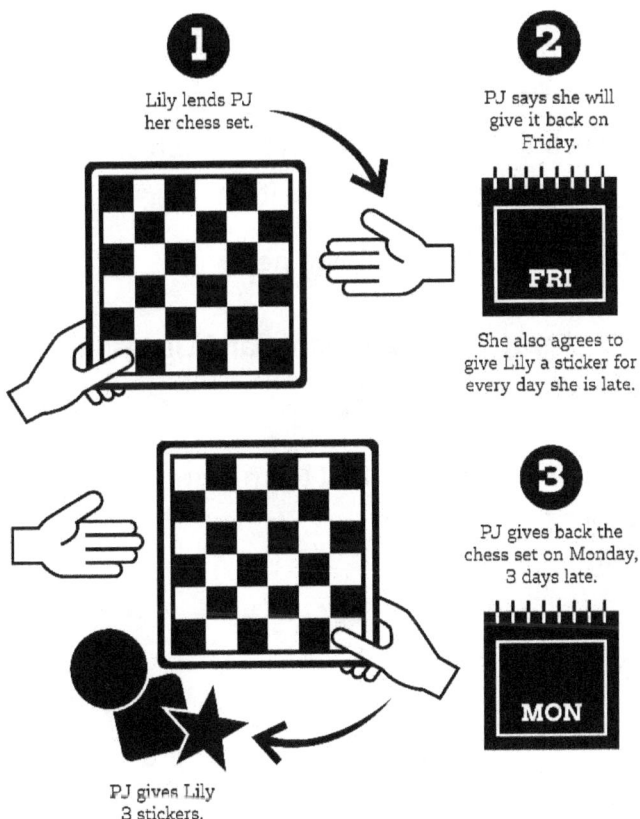

Lily's eyes light up. "So the longer she keeps my game, the more stickers I get? That's so cool!" She pauses, her excitement fading. "Wait... but PJ would hate that. She loves her stickers."

Jamie nods energetically, leaning forward. "That's how interest works. If you don't pay the bank back on time, they make you pay extra money—kind of like giving up stickers. And nobody likes that."

Mom chuckles as she stands, picking up her plate. "Nobody wants to give the bank extra money—especially after working so hard to earn it."

Jamie nods, his mom's words sinking in. He puts his napkin on his plate and stares at the ceiling. A credit card seems like a good idea, but the idea of paying interest still makes him uneasy. Is he really ready to take it on?

What do you think he should do next?

OPTION 1: Apply for a credit card. Jamie is ready. HEAD TO COMMENCING CREDIT - PAGE 11

OPTION 2: He should wait and learn more. HEAD TO FINANCIAL FOUNDATIONS - PAGE 13

COMMENCING CREDIT

The following week, Jamie applies for a credit card online. The application asks for stuff like his name, address, workplace, and how much he earns. Jamie's eyes settle on the '**income**' section—he only started working at Sundae Sanctuary a few months ago—but a grin creeps onto his face as he types in an actual number for the first time. He's earning money!

A few days later, the bank approves his application and mails the credit card to his house. When it arrives, Jamie holds it up, admiring his name printed right there on the shiny plastic. He reads the letter it came with and learns that his starting **credit limit** is $2,500. He can't help but feel a mix of excitement and responsibility as he reads it.

A week later, Max decides to do the same. Jamie walks him through the process, but Max is only half paying attention, his eyes glued to a rerun of his favorite show on TV. "Easy peasy, Jamie," he says.

"You spelled your name wrong," Jamie jokes, making Max do a double take.

When Max's card arrives in the mail, the two friends feel like they've hit a big milestone. "Finally," Max says, flipping his card over in his hands. "I don't have to wait for my next paycheck!"

Jamie laughs, though a flicker of doubt lingers—is Max ready for this?

HEAD TO A WALK TO WISDOM- PAGE 15

FINANCIAL FOUNDATIONS

Jamie spends the rest of his Saturday afternoon lounging on the couch, scrolling through his phone. He rests his arm over his eyes and his earlier conversation with his parents keeps replaying in his head. Maybe he isn't ready for a credit card just yet.

He signs up for a free, highly-rated online class called "Financial Foundations: Build Your Future."

The next day, Jamie settles at the dining room table with his laptop and a notebook. The screen flickers to life, and a friendly face appears: Mrs. Kelly, the course instructor. She's a retired banker with silver-streaked hair and glasses perched on the tip of her nose. Her smile is warm and inviting.

"Welcome, everyone," Mrs. Kelly begins, her energetic voice creating a friendly atmosphere. Jamie sees other participants smile. He leans closer to the screen.

Throughout the course, Mrs. Kelly talks about money using relatable examples. "Think of your money like a pie," she says, and a chart flashes on the screen. "Each slice represents something important—like saving for college, saving for emergencies, or fun money. If you eat all the slices now, there won't be any left for later."

Then, she talks about mindless spending, showing how small purchases can quietly add up. Jamie catches sight of the snack wrappers in his bag from the vending machine at school. Guilty.

As the session wraps up, Mrs. Kelly leaves them with a final piece of advice. "Financial success isn't about being perfect. It's about making small, consistent choices that move you closer to your goals." For the first time, he sees money not as something to be afraid of, but as something he can control.

By the end of the day, Jamie feels ready. The idea of a credit card doesn't seem as overwhelming anymore.

HEAD TO COMMENCING CREDIT- PAGE 11

A WALK TO WISDOM

It is another beautiful day in Maplewood. Jamie's family decides to take a walk into town, enjoying the sunlight streaming through the tree-lined paths. Lily skips energetically ahead, but then spins around to face her family with a thoughtful look. "Mom, I still don't get credit cards. Why don't people just use the money they have instead of borrowing it from the bank?"

"That's a great question, Lily," Mom says with a smile. "One big reason is convenience. I can buy things with my credit card without carrying a lot of cash."

As they walk, the sounds of downtown Maplewood fill the air—the hum of passing cars and the chatter of diners enjoying their meals outside. They pass colorful storefronts, and Lily's eyes light up as they reach a bike shop. In the front window, a shiny, bright blue bike catches her attention.

"Look! That's the bike I want for my birthday!" she exclaims, pointing eagerly.

Mom slips her arm through Lily's. "Hey, that's a great bike!" They walk closer to the window to take a better look. Mom says, "OK, let's pretend we decided to buy it today, but I didn't bring enough money. A credit card would let us buy the bike right now. The bank pays the bike store for us, and then I pay the bank back later."

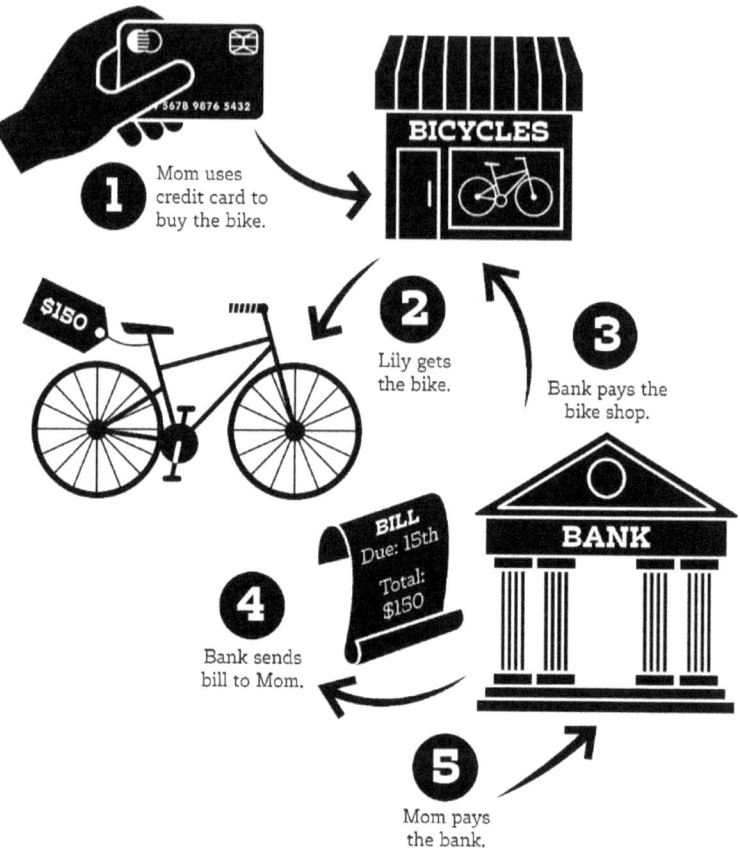

Dad chimes in as they continue their stroll. "And remember last year at the airport? I used my credit card to book a hotel online when our flight was canceled."

Lily glances back at the bikes again before looking around at the lively street. "So, credit cards can help if you don't have money with you, or you need to shop online?"

Jamie grins and nudges her playfully. "Look at my genius little sister! Next thing you know, you'll be running the family **finances** and charging me rent!"

A Walk to Wisdom

"Ha!" Lily says. "You better start saving now!"

As they near their house, Jamie throws an arm around Lily. "Hey, you wanna play that new video game we got last week? And while we play, I can tell you about something called credit scores."

Lily shoots him a competitive grin. "Prepare for defeat! I'm going to beat your high score *and* learn about credit scores. Double win!"

They race each other up the driveway, laughter echoing as they head inside, ready for both fun and a little learning.

FLIP TO THE NEXT PAGE.

SCORING POINTS

Lily and Jamie flop onto the couch, controllers ready, as the game loads. Soon, their players dart across the screen, dodging alien traps and collecting glowing gems. Jamie's fingers fly over the buttons, his eyes locked on the action.

"Bet you're just gonna use your credit card to buy more games," Lily teases, her player leaping ahead of his.

Jamie smirks, pausing the game mid-jump. "You think so, huh?" He turns to face her. "Credit cards aren't just for buying stuff, you know."

Lily raises an eyebrow. "Well what else are they for?"

"They're also a way to build your credit score," Jamie says, motioning to the screen with the controller. "And it works kind of like this game."

"Okay, now you've lost me," Lily says, sinking into the couch.

Jamie nods. "In this video game, I'm trying to rack up points to get a high score, right? It's the same idea with a **credit score**. But instead of collecting gems, I can earn points by using my credit card."

Lily blinks. "You get points for spending money?"

"Not exactly," Jamie says, leaning back. "You get points for using your credit card *the right way*—only buying what you can afford and always paying it back on time. And the higher your score, the more cool stuff you can get later. Like being able to borrow money to buy a house. Think of it like unlocking real-life bonus levels."

"Wait—real-life bonus levels? It sounds like secret treasure!" Lily sits up, eyes wide.

Jamie shakes his head and laughs. "More like—with a good credit score, banks and stores trust you more and are willing to lend you money. But if you miss payments, your score drops, and they think you're bad at managing it."

"Who's controlling all these points? Is there a Credit Boss?"

Jamie chuckles. "No. There are these companies called credit bureaus, and they are like scorekeepers. They update your score based on how you handle your bills. Mess up, and it can take years to recover."

Lily's face twists in horror. "Years? That's worse than forgetting to hit save before you exit your game!"

"Way worse," Jamie says with a nod. "Remember cousin Sarah? She got her first credit card and was all excited, but she missed quite a few payments. Her credit score tanked, and she couldn't get a **loan** when she really needed a new car. She was stuck with her old, unreliable one for a long time."

Lily frowns. "That sounds bad. I don't want that to happen to you."

Jamie nudges her shoulder, smiling. "Relax, Lil. I've got this."

Lily taps her controller thoughtfully. "So when can you start earning these points?"

Jamie shrugs. "Soon. That's why I wanted a credit card now. The longer you use it right, the better your score gets."

Lily grins mischievously. "Okay, enough about credit scores. Let's get back to *my* high score." She presses a button, unpausing the game.

"Hey!" Jamie shouts, diving back into the action. "No fair starting without me!"

Lily lets out a belly laugh. "You might get a good credit score soon, but I'll have the high score here!"

FLIP TO THE NEXT PAGE.

GAME ON!

One Friday after school, Max and Jamie decide to visit the Maplewood Arcade.

As they walk through the busy rooms, with lights flashing and games whirling, Max's eyes beam with excitement. "Jamie, check out the new 'Diamond Zone' game! It just came out. We could be the first ones to play it here!"

Jamie stops mid-step, his eyes immediately landing on the game console. "No way! I didn't know it was out already. Let's do it!"

They drop their backpacks near a pair of empty chairs and step up to the game.

Jamie pulls a crumpled twenty-dollar bill from his pocket and feeds it into the cash slot. Max does the same. The machines kick off with a blast of music, and soon they're navigating their characters through a maze of wormholes and tunnels, shouting instructions and cheering each other on.

After three intense rounds, Jamie's screen flashes 'Game Over.' He checks his pockets and groans. "Man, this game eats up money fast!" He stands and stretches. "I'm out. What about you?"

Max pats his own pockets, coming up empty too. His hand hovers briefly before he pulls out his wallet. His fingers brush the edge of his new credit card. He glances at the game's glowing screen, then at the empty chair that Jamie was now walking away from. His heart races a little, excitement battling with uncertainty.

"I don't have any more cash, but I'll just use the credit card for a few more games." Max says, though his voice comes out quieter than he expects. "I want to get past a few more rounds."

Jamie, halfway to their backpacks, stops and turns. "Careful, Max. This game seems like a money vacuum."

Max shifts uncomfortably, chewing his lip. Without looking at Jamie, he slides the card into the slot. *It's just an arcade game*, he thinks. *How bad could it be?*

"Just a few more rounds," he mutters.

The sounds of the arcade swell around them as Max continues to play. Jamie stays quiet, leaning against the console with his arms crossed. After a while, Max pauses the game and checks the total.

"Whoa. I've already spent fifty bucks," he says, his voice tight.

Jamie casts a sideways glance. "Ouch. Maybe we should head out, get some fresh air or something."

Max stares blankly at the screen. He feels stuck, as if the game and his new card are daring him to make a choice. What do you think he should do?

OPTION 1: Stop Playing- he's spent enough already. HEAD TO DAMAGE CONTROL- PAGE 25

OPTION 2: Keep Playing- a few more rounds won't hurt. HEAD TO DIAMOND DISASTER- PAGE 27

DAMAGE CONTROL

Max has had enough. He steps back from the game console, his fingers lingering for a moment before pulling away. Jamie follows close behind, and together they weave through the noisy chaos of the arcade toward the exit.

Once outside, Max lets out a long breath. The cool air hits his face, a sharp contrast to the arcade's muggy warmth. He feels his shoulders relax as the tension starts to melt away.

"Fifty bucks," Max mutters, shaking his head. "I didn't even realize how fast it added up. Using a credit card makes it feel like fake money." He stuffs his hands into his hoodie pockets.

Jamie nods, sliding sunglasses from his backpack onto his face. "Totally. Swiping a card doesn't feel like spending cash—it's way too easy to lose track."

Max kicks a small rock on the sidewalk, sending it skidding ahead of them. "Good thing I've got a job. I can cover it with my next paycheck. But still..." His voice trails off as he looks down at his sneakers.

Jamie stays quiet, giving Max space to think.

After a moment, Max speaks again, his voice steadier. "At least I stopped before it got worse. I mean, I could've kept going, but I didn't. That's gotta count for something, right?"

Jamie grins and nudges Max's arm. "For sure. You noticed what was happening and stopped. That's the whole point—being in control, not letting the card run the show."

As they near Max's house, he pulls his credit card from his pocket, examining it as if it were a strange relic. "This little thing," he says with a smirk, "can do a lot of damage if you're not careful."

Jamie nods. "Yeah, but now you know better. Lesson learned."

Max chuckles, slipping the card back into his wallet. "Guess I've still got a lot to learn." He pauses at his front door and glances at Jamie. "Thanks for having my back, man. I needed that."

Jamie shrugs. "What are friends for? Besides saving you from yourself at the arcade?"

Max laughs as he pushes the door open. "Right. See you tomorrow."

Max leans against the door as it clicks shut. He made a mistake, sure, but he also made the choice to stop. Maybe he was starting to figure out this whole responsibility thing after all.

HEAD TO TECH TEMPTATION- PAGE 29

DIAMOND DISASTER

Max is still deciding when he glances over Jamie's shoulder and spots a group of their friends walking into the arcade. A grin spreads across his face as he waves them over.

"Hey, guys! Jamie and I were just playing the new 'Diamond Zone' game. Check it out!"

Their friends crowd around, eyes lighting up as they see the flashing screen. "Whoa, you're so close to the high score!" one of them says, nudging Max.

That's all it takes. Max grabs his credit card again, holding it for a moment as the game screen flashes. He feels the weight of Jamie's eyes on him. "I'll just play a few more rounds," Max mutters, sliding the card into the slot before Jamie can reply.

Jamie doesn't stop him, but walks away from the machine and leans against a wall. He pulls out his phone.

After a while, Jamie speaks up, keeping his tone casual. "You know, this game's got a reputation for eating people's money. It only just came out and people are already referring to it as 'Die-Money Zone'." Jamie continues to thumb through articles.

Max pauses mid-swipe and gives Jamie the side-eye.

Jamie shrugs. "I'm just saying. There's even a post about people spending hundreds to try to beat the high score."

Finally, the screen flashes GAME OVER, and Max steps back, rubbing the back of his neck. He then sees the damage. $120 — spent.

He swallows hard. "I didn't think we played *that* many games."

Jamie doesn't say "I told you so." Instead, he claps a hand on Max's shoulder. "Come on. Let's get out of here."

As they leave the arcade and start the walk home, Max stares at the pavement, his thoughts racing. "Man, it's way too easy to spend money with that credit card," he says finally, breaking the silence.

Jamie nods. "I get it. When you don't see the cash leaving your wallet, it doesn't feel like spending real money."

Max sighs. "Yeah, no kidding. Now I'm stuck with this huge bill. And for what?" He stares at the ground, frustration creeping in. "I could've spent that money on something that actually mattered."

NEXT PAGE.

TECH TEMPTATION

A month later, after Max pays off his first **credit card bill** using the money from his paycheck, Jamie, Max, and a few friends walk to the local tech store, which buzzes with the energy of young, excited shoppers. As they enter, their eyes dart to the center of the store where the latest TechUltra Laptop shines under the spotlight on a rotating display.

This laptop is everything. It boasts a top-tier graphics processor perfect for Jamie's digital art and Max's gaming needs, it's incredibly lightweight, and it has an exceptional 20-hour battery life. Not to mention the customizable LED keyboard—it's amazing!

"That's the one we were looking at for college!" Max says, nudging Jamie toward the laptop. "We could just buy it now, right? We've got our magic card!" His voice carries a mix of excitement and a dash of mischief.

Jamie chuckles at his friend's enthusiasm but feels a tug of caution. "It's tempting," he admits, his gaze lingering on the sleek design, "but I haven't saved up enough to buy it yet. It's $2,000. That's no small chunk of change."

Leaning in, Max's voice drops to a whisper. "But imagine walking out of here today with that laptop." His fingers twitch toward his pocket as he pictures carrying it home, already dreaming of gaming marathons and school projects on his new toy.

"And imagine walking out with a heap of interest if you can't pay it back," Jamie quips, snapping Max out of his fantasy.

Max pauses. "Well, maybe you can't buy it, but that doesn't mean I can't." He smirks. "Besides, you're starting to sound like my grandma," he adds with a laugh, though he hasn't even mentioned the credit card to her.

Jamie shakes his head, deciding to take a different approach. "Hey, remember the drone you bought last summer with your birthday money?" he asks, a playful edge creeping into his voice.

Max rolls his eyes but can't hide a sheepish grin. "Okay, but you've gotta admit—that thing was awesome."

"True," Jamie says, grinning. "But where is it now?"

Max lets out a reluctant laugh. "Somewhere at the bottom of the lake. How was I supposed to know it'd crash so easily?" He sighs, running his hand through his hair. "Okay, fine. You're right. It *was* an **impulse** purchase. But this laptop is different."

Tech Temptation

Jamie tilts his head. "Is it? Maybe you should do some research first, see if it's really the best one for you—or wait until there's a sale?"

Then, lowering his voice, Jamie adds, "Do you even have enough saved?" He watches as Max's expression shifts, the gears turning in his head.

Jamie lightens the mood, "Or maybe you can work triple shifts at Sundae Sanctuary to cover it. You can flex your scooping muscles."

Max lets out a short laugh. He pictures himself walking into school with the sleek laptop in his bag, but the thought of working multiple shifts suddenly doesn't sound so fun.

What will Max say?

OPTION 1: "I'll wait and save up—it's the smart move." Head to Financial Flashback- Page 33

OPTION 2: "I'm buying it now—I'll handle the bill later!" Head to The Impulse Purchase- Page 53

FINANCIAL FLASHBACK

Max and Jamie walk out of the store and part ways with their friends. After a moment, Max turns to Jamie with a grin, a genuine look of relief in his eyes.

"OK, now that we're out of there, I'm realizing how dumb it would've been to actually buy that laptop today." He exhales and rubs the back of his neck.

"You know," he continues slowly, "I had a flashback in the store. A memory of my uncle Joe. He had a huge issue with credit card payments. I remember him telling my grandma that he couldn't afford to pay anything back except the interest. I remember him yelling it, actually. He looked so stressed all the time, like he couldn't catch a break. Once, he even sold his guitar to make a payment. That guitar was his favorite thing in the world."

Jamie's eyes widen. "So, what happened?"

"All I know is that it took years for him to get out of his mess. I remember him saying he was stuck. It's funny how you remember things like that."

Jamie nods, his gaze lingering on Max. "Yeah, that's the thing about interest. You're basically running in place if that's all you pay. It's brutal."

"What do you mean?"

"Well, let's say your uncle spent $5,000 buying a bunch of things. So his **debt**, or what he owed the bank, was $5,000, right? But if he could only afford to pay back the interest, that means he was never actually able to pay back any part of that $5,000. And the longer it takes to pay it off, the more interest piles up. It's like digging a hole you can't climb out of."

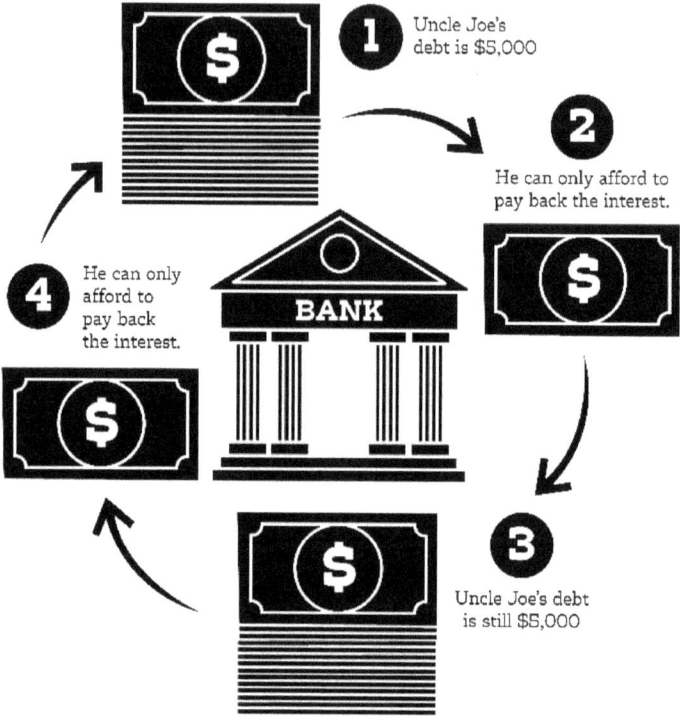

"That sounds awful," Max says. "I definitely don't want to go down that road." His voice trails off as he glances away. "Or make my grandma worry like he did."

Jamie puts a hand on Max's shoulder. "You won't. You're already way ahead of most people—plus, I won't let you become Uncle Joe 2.0."

Max nods, feeling strangely better. "Thanks, Jamie. It took me a minute but I'm glad I made the right call."

NEXT PAGE.

SCOOPS AND SAVINGS

A few days after their visit to the Tech store, Jamie and Max decide to shift their focus to **budgeting**, to track how much they earn and how much they can save for the laptop. This way, they'll know exactly how much money they will have in a few months, and will know when they'll be able to afford it.

They both work at Sundae Sanctuary on the days they're free after school, where the air inside is always thick with the smell of freshly baked waffle cones and vanilla.

During their shifts, Max expertly scoops ice cream into confectionary cones for eager customers. Jamie, wiping down the tables, often finds his apron speckled with colorful sprinkles. As they work, they chat about their savings goals, each scoop and each cleaned table bringing them a step closer to their dream laptop.

They also decide to take up side jobs; Jamie starts tutoring on the weekends, helping younger kids with math and science, while Max starts walking dogs in the neighborhood.

One day, during a lull at the shop, Max and Jamie discuss their savings goals again.

"So, our **income** is about a thousand dollars each month now, right?" Jamie asks. He glances over at Max who nods, concentrating on the waffle cone stack he's preparing for display.

"Yep, that's right," Max says. "In two months, we'll each have $2,000 saved up, and we can both buy the TechUltra."

Jamie pauses, wiping his hands on his apron. "Actually, I was thinking… maybe instead of putting all our savings toward the laptop, we could set aside some of it for other things—just in case of an emergency or something."

"An emergency?" asks Max, looking up. "What kind of emergencies do you think we'll get ourselves into?"

"None, hopefully!" Jamie chuckles, grabbing a spray bottle. "But think about it—what if my laptop gets stolen, or your phone breaks? Stuff like that happens, and we'd be scrambling without a backup plan."

Max, finishing his arrangement of the waffle cones, turns to face Jamie. "It's not *just* a laptop, Jamie. It's like… having something amazing to show for all this hard work. Can't we start saving for emergencies after we get it?"

Jamie taps his finger against his lip. "I get it, Max. The laptop is a big deal. But wouldn't it feel even better knowing we're not totally broke if something goes wrong? Hear me out. What if we put, say, sixty percent into the laptop **fund**, and save forty percent for the unexpected? So, if we save $1,000 this month, that's $600 for the laptop and $400 for emergencies."

Max shakes his head with a small smile, clearly eager to reach their goal as soon as possible. "Let's make it ninety-ten, Jamie. Ten percent for 'emergencies'—that's still something, right?"

Scoops and Savings

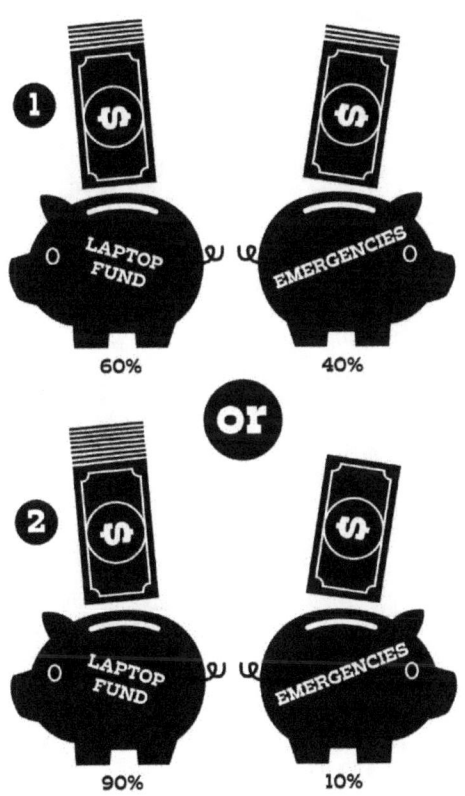

Jamie gives it some thought. Max does make a compelling argument. He tries to decide which budget to choose.

Option 1: 60% to the laptop fund and 40% to the emergency fund. HEAD TO A CUSHION FOR CRISIS- PAGE 39

Option 2: 90% to the laptop fund and 10% to the emergency fund. HEAD TO CONCERT CONUNDRUM- PAGE 43

A CUSHION FOR CRISIS

But Jamie insists. "Max, I really think it'll be smart if we start saving for other things besides the laptop, too. I'm serious."

Jamie grabs a napkin and starts sketching out numbers. "Okay, look," he says, holding it up. "If we put $400 aside every month, in just three months, that's $1,200. Enough to handle something big if it comes up—like, I don't know, your phone falling in the lake."

Max snorts, grabbing the napkin to scribble a quick doodle of a sinking phone. "Your phone, more like." He knocks on the counter. "Okay, let's try your way. It will only be a few more months."

Over the next three months, Jamie and Max stick to their plan. They continue to earn about $1,000 each month and split their earnings, with 60% funneled into their laptop **fund** and 40% into an "emergency" fund. By the end of three months, they've both accumulated $1,800 for the laptop and $1,200 in their emergency reserve.

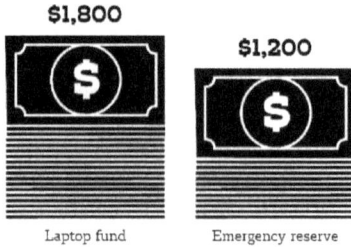

One chilly Saturday, as Max is finishing up a dog-walking session, his phone buzzes with an unexpected call. It's the local hospital. His heart sinks as he answers, immediately worried about his grandmother.

"Hello, this is Max. Is everything okay?"

The nurse on the other end explains, "Hi Max, I'm calling about your grandmother. She had a minor fall, and we brought her here as a precaution. She's stable, but she will need a few tests and possibly some minor treatment. Could you come to the hospital?"

Max is relieved it's not more serious. "I'll be right there. Thank you."

At the hospital, after seeing that his grandmother is okay but will need some follow-up care, Max speaks with the billing desk. "We'll need a payment for today's visit," the receptionist says, sliding a form across the counter. Max nods and pulls out his wallet, his mind flashing to the emergency fund he's been building. For the first time, he feels like it's all been worth it.

Later, sitting beside his grandmother's hospital bed, Max leans forward and gently takes her hand. "Grandma. I want you to focus on getting yourself better. I'll take care of the medical bills."

A Cushion for Crisis

Her frail fingers tighten around his hand, her skin soft but cool. Max sees a glisten in her eye as she whispers, "Max, you've grown into such a thoughtful, responsible young man."

Max swallows the lump in his throat and smiles. "Thanks, Grandma."

Once she's settled and resting, Max steps into the quiet hospital corridor and dials Jamie. "Jamie, it happened. I actually had to use the emergency fund. Grandma had a fall, but she's okay."

Jamie's voice sharpens after a brief pause. "Hold on, what? Is she alright?"

"Yeah, she's stable. It's nothing major, just some tests and follow-up stuff," Max says, leaning against the wall. "But I was able to pay for it. That fund literally saved me."

Jamie lets out a long breath. "Man, I'm so glad you had it. And let me know if she needs anything, okay?"

Max leans his head back against the wall, exhaling. "Yeah, I will. Thanks, Jamie."

A few days later, back at Sundae Sanctuary, Max and Jamie reflect on everything while going about their usual work routine. Max scoops ice cream, his movements slow, the cold metal handle biting against his palm. He stares into the tub for a moment. "You know, Jamie, I was always so focused on getting that laptop…" he says, his voice quieter than usual. He leans against the counter, his hands lingering on the ice cream scoop.

For once, the memory of his emergency fund doesn't sting—it feels like the best decision he's ever made.

Jamie looks at his friend and no further words need to be spoken.

Head to Path to Prosperity- Page 49

CONCERT CONUNDRUM

Reluctantly, Jamie nods. After all, $100 a month is better than nothing. "Fine, we'll follow your suggestion with a ninety-ten split then. But let's review it in a few months, okay?"

Over the next two months, Jamie and Max follow their plan. Their earnings from Sundae Sanctuary and their side jobs accumulate, and they diligently divide the money according to their **budget**. They set aside $900 for the laptop and $100 for emergencies and other things each month.

Their laptop fund grows to $1,800, and a smaller, separate fund of $200 slowly starts to take shape.

One brisk Saturday afternoon, as they discuss plans for the summer, Max's phone buzzes with an alert. He checks it, and his face lights up. "No way! This is awesome!" He springs up from his stool. "The Solar Vibes are coming to town next weekend for a surprise performance! Tickets went on sale this morning!"

A thrill of excitement rushes through Jamie. Solar Vibes is his favorite band. He and his friends memorized every song back in middle school and spent countless hours debating which albums had the best solos.

"Dude, we have to go," Jamie says. "How much are the tickets?"

Max spends a minute scrolling on his phone. Jamie hears him mutter, "Uh-oh, the cheap seats are already sold out." Max scrolls some more, then says, "The only tickets left are $350 or more. That is steep!"

Jamie slouches onto a stool and leans his head into his hands. He'd spend $350 in a heartbeat to see Solar Vibes live, but their budget is tight. "Max, I hate to say it, but I wish we had put more into our other savings fund. We only have $200 in there."

Max scratches the back of his neck, his brows furrowing as he glances at the screen again. He holds his breath, his thumb repeatedly tapping the refresh button as if the price might magically change.

"Okay, you were right," he says. "Man, I hate having to choose between stuff like this and saving." He glances at Jamie. "But maybe we can figure something out. Thank goodness this isn't an actual emergency."

NEXT PAGE.

FUN AND FUNDS

After some serious thought, Max and Jamie decide to go for it and buy tickets to see Solar Vibes, using some money from their laptop fund. They realize it might be their last chance to rock out together with all their friends before everyone heads off to college—a final hurrah to cap off their high school days.

When the concert night arrives, it surpasses all their expectations. The venue is electric, buzzing with the energy of a crowd in perfect harmony. Their friends are all there, and as the band takes the stage, everyone sings along at the top of their lungs. It's an unforgettable evening, and though the tickets were expensive, the memories, they agree, are truly priceless.

A few days later, still buzzing from the excitement of the concert, Max and Jamie sit down to talk about their budget again. They realize they need to make some changes to avoid a similar situation in the future.

"The concert was a blast," Max says. "But dipping into our laptop savings to pay for it was kind of a bummer."

"I feel the same way," Jamie says, thinking for a moment. Then he pulls out a notebook and proposes a solution. "How about we reorganize our budget into better savings buckets now? We could have one for the laptop, one for emergencies, and one for college stuff we'll need, like books and supplies. This way, we'll be more prepared for college and any real emergency that might come up."

Max nods in agreement. "That's smart. We've got all sorts of **expenses** coming up with college. Let's make sure we plan for that."

As Jamie sketches out the plan, they divide their savings: 50% for the laptop fund, 30% for emergencies, and 20% for college expenses. "We're going to be the most prepared college kids ever," Jamie says.

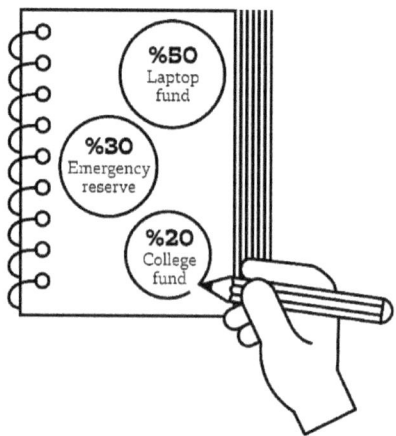

"You got that right," Max says, a grin spreading across his face. "And after we've saved enough for our laptops, we can change it and create a new fund for fun stuff."

Their new budget makes them feel prepared for what's to come, and within a few months, the first wave of emails from their university confirms they are on the right track. The emails list the textbooks they need and the supplies required for their fall classes. One of their professors even sends out an assignment to start over the summer.

Fun and Funds

Jamie and Max realize that with the TechUltra laptop, which they can now afford, they are equipped to tackle the assignment right away. They also manage to buy all the other supplies they need without touching their emergency funds.

"I'll say it again," Max reflects one day. "Looking back, I'm glad we went to the concert. It taught us that we can have fun and still hit our goals, just by planning a bit."

The two learn that budgeting isn't about sacrificing all the fun; it's about striking a balance between enjoying the present and preparing for the future.

Hooray, you've made it to the end of this journey! What would you like to do next?

- **Go back and see what happens if they decide to create a bigger emergency fund. How might planning ahead prepare them for the unexpected?**
  HEAD TO A CUSHION FOR CRISIS- PAGE 39

- **See what happens if Max chooses to buy the laptop right away. Is he prepared to manage his payments?**
  HEAD TO THE IMPULSE PURCHASE- PAGE 53

Or, if you're ready, head to END OF OUR ADVENTURE- PAGE 75

PATH TO PROSPERITY

Many months after Max's grandmother's fall, life has settled back into its usual rhythm in Maplewood. The sound of laughter fills the Sundae Sanctuary as Max jokes with Jamie during their shifts, while weekends are now spent planning (and saving!) for college or strolling through the bustling downtown. Even the simple act of walking past the arcade reminds Max of how far they've come. Max and Jamie, now just weeks away from high school graduation, continue to apply the lessons they've learned about budgeting and spending wisely.

On another bright Saturday morning, the town of Maplewood buzzes with the excitement of the annual Community Fair. Max and Jamie are looking forward to a fun day out, but first, Jamie is ready to buy his first car and asks Max to come along for support.

"Look at us now!" Max exclaims, grinning. "Saving for that laptop taught us a lot. I'm glad we stuck with our budget even when it was tough. And now you're off to get a car!"

At the car dealership, Jamie fidgets with the edge of his jacket, tapping his fingers excitedly on his lap.

His parents' generous graduation gift, enough to help with the car's **down payment**, flashes in his mind. This, along with the money he's saved up from his jobs, makes Jamie feel ready to buy a car. He's also planning to **finance** a portion of the car through the dealership's **loan** program, which will help him build his credit further.

Just then, a car salesman walks over with a warm smile.

"Good morning, young men. My name is Adam—glad to have you in the showroom. How can I help you today?"

"I'm here to buy my first car," Jamie says.

"Congratulations!" Adam says, clasping his hands together. "I'll be happy to help with that. The first thing we'll need to do is run a **credit check** to see the financing options for you."

Jamie provides him with the information that is requested. In under a half hour, Jamie receives his **credit report** back, which leaves Adam looking impressed.

"Well, you have a solid credit score, Jamie," he says. "And that means you qualify for favorable **interest rates**."

Jamie's eyes widen, and a grin spreads across his face. He can't wait to tell Lily that his good credit score finally unlocked 'the next level'.

"That's amazing! Now I can save more money and put it toward college expenses."

In this moment, though he's not buying a car, Max feels a warm sense of pride. He catches himself smiling as he remembers how he'd struggled at the arcade months ago. *Man*, he thinks, *I've really turned things around.* Taking control of his spending habits now feels like a milestone he wasn't sure he'd reach.

Path to Prosperity

Later, the boys spend the day enjoying the fair with their friends, filled with a new sense of accomplishment. They play games, eat cotton candy, and take a few thrilling rides. The evening air is filled with laughter and the glow of twinkling lights as the sun goes down.

As they sit on a bench overlooking the field, Max shares his next goal with Jamie.

"You know, I've been thinking a lot about Grandma lately. She's done so much for me. I am going to start putting aside some money to help her, in case she needs anything while I'm away at school."

Jamie nods and turns to Max, his smile widening.

The boys stand and head toward Jamie's new car, a sense of independence filling the air.

"Hey. Having good credit doesn't just help with buying a car," he says. "It's going to be a big help next year when we want to rent an apartment."

"And when I start my own custom gaming shop one day," Max says with a small smile, "my credit score will help me get the loan I need for tools and supplies. Imagine it—custom controllers, keyboards, and headsets. How cool would that be?"

He raises an imaginary glass in cheers. "To good choices, great friends, and all the adventures ahead!"

Jamie laughs, joining in. "To good credit scores and all the doors they open!"

Great job! You've made it to the end of this journey! What would you like to do next?

- **Go back and see what happens if they decide to create a smaller emergency fund. Will they be caught unprepared?** HEAD TO CONCERT CONUNDRUM- PAGE 43

- **See what happens if Max chooses to buy the laptop right away. Is he prepared to manage his payments?** HEAD TO THE IMPULSE PURCHASE- PAGE 53

    Or, if you're ready, head to END OF OUR ADVENTURE- PAGE 75

THE IMPULSE PURCHASE

Max's gaze is locked on the sleek TechUltra Laptop, his ears buzzing with a mix of excitement and Jamie's words of caution. The cool, metallic surface feels smooth under his fingertips, and he barely notices the salesperson named Amanda approaching with a warm smile.

"This model's been flying off the shelves. Everyone's raving about its performance. Honestly, we can't keep these in stock. Better grab it quick—these don't stick around," she says with a wink.

Amanda's words hang in the air, tempting him like bait on a hook. Max hesitates for just a moment before pulling out his credit card.

"I'll take it," he says, the rush of adrenaline sending a jolt through his fingers as he hands it over.

"You're going to love it—great choice!" Amanda says. She completes the transaction and walks the bag containing the laptop around the counter, handing it to Max. He takes it and grips the handles tightly, and for a moment, he can't stop grinning.

But as they head towards the exit, a wave of unease begins to creep in. When they step outside, Max clutches the bag like it might vanish. "This is... going to be great for college!" is all he could think to say, his voice trailing off.

Jamie glances at the bag. "It's a killer laptop, no doubt. Just make sure you've got a plan to pay it off. You're, um, pretty close to hitting your credit limit."

Max shifts the bag to his other hand, the handles suddenly digging into his fingers. "Yeah, I know. I'll figure it out." His voice is steady, but Jamie doesn't miss the way his eyes dart to the ground.

Jamie doesn't say anything, but as they walk away, he catches the way Max keeps shifting the bag, as if the weight of it is already more than he bargained for. He can't help but wonder how long the excitement will outlast the reality of paying it off.

NEXT PAGE.

DEBT DILEMMA

Over the next few weeks, Max spends a lot of time on his TechUltra. Between late-night homework sessions and catching up on his favorite shows, the laptop quickly becomes his go-to companion.

When the credit card bill arrives the next month, Max feels a knot in his stomach. He tears it open and immediately spots the laptop charge. There it is, plain as day—a reminder of how much he owes.

"What was I thinking, dropping over two thousand dollars?" he mutters, holding the bill in both hands. His chest tightens as reality sinks in—his part-time job at Sundae Sanctuary won't even make a dent in this. He exhales, slumping into his chair.

When he looks at the bill more closely, he sees it says he can pay a **minimum due** of $40. "Okay, I can afford this," he reassures himself, and logs into his account online.

As Max hovers over the "Pay $40 Minimum" option, Jamie's voice echoes in his mind. He remembers a lazy afternoon in Jamie's living room, watching him lean over his own credit card bill.

"See this? The Total **Balance**—everything I owe," Jamie had said, tapping the page. Then he pointed to the fine print. "And here? Minimum Due. It's the smallest amount you can pay, but it barely covers the interest. It's a trap. If you only pay this, you'll end up owing even more later. Trust me, it's not worth it."

Max heeds Jamie's phantom advice and pays $600 instead of the minimum $40. It drains most of his savings, leaving him uneasy. But he knows the alternative—racking up even more interest—would feel worse in the long run.

You're smart. You can handle this, he thinks, sitting up straighter.

With the weather warming up, the Sundae Sanctuary buzzes with customers. Max asks to work more shifts scooping ice cream, each chime of the register reminding him of his growing savings.

After only a week, though, the excitement of the approaching summer makes him forget about his laptop payments and sweeps him into a flurry of unexpected spending.

At Maplewood Amusement Park, the smell of popcorn and funnel cakes tempts him, and before long, he's buying souvenirs and snacks for his friends. He even splurges on pool outings.

At first, Max comes home feeling exhilarated, often falling asleep with memories of the day replaying in his head.

Soon, however, sleep begins to escape him. The weight of his carefree spending presses harder with every passing day as he tosses uncomfortably in bed.

It all comes crashing down one evening when he reviews his next credit card bill. His eyes scan the list: amusement park tickets ($100), snacks and souvenirs ($60), pool time ($40)— each one a small indulgence that's added up fast.

Debt Dilemma

And of course, there's the remainder of his laptop ($1,400) looming at the bottom like a weight pulling him under.

One afternoon, while hanging out at Jamie's house, Max glances at the table and sees Jamie's opened bill lying on top of a stack of mail. His balance is neat and manageable, nothing like the mess Max has built up.

He wishes he could be like Jamie. Should he swallow his pride and ask for advice, or try to handle the mess himself?

OPTION 1: Yes—Max decides to ask Jamie for advice. HEAD TO CONVERSATIONS AND CHOICES- PAGE 59

OPTION 2: No—Max chooses to tackle the problem on his own. HEAD TO THE SILENT STRUGGLE- PAGE 67

CONVERSATIONS AND CHOICES

Rain drips steadily outside as Max and Jamie return from basketball and settle in the kitchen. Max fidgets with the strap of his bag as he debates when to say something. The words feel like rocks in his mouth.

Suddenly, they tumble out before he can stop them: "Jamie, I've messed up. I've been spending way too much with my credit card..."

Jamie's hand freezes mid-reach for a water bottle. His brows draw together as he looks over and studies Max's face.

He straightens up, his water bottle forgotten, and turns to face Max. "Okay," his voice is calm. "What's been going on?"

Max swallows hard, his posture stiffening before he finally speaks again. "Well, I spent that stupid amount at the arcade the first week we got the card, but I paid all that back. Then, I got the laptop, and you were right, Jamie. It's too much."

Jamie slowly takes a seat on a stool and rubs his hands over his knees.

Max continues, "I used my $600 in savings to pay the balance down, but then... I just kept spending."

Max rubs his eyes with his palms, his voice breaking slightly. "I don't know what's wrong with me. I just... I can't seem to stop. Now it's back up to $1,800. What am I supposed to do?"

Jamie takes a sip of water and clears his throat. "How much did you say your balance was?"

"$1,800," Max says, staring at the floor.

After a moment, Jamie stands and squeezes Max's shoulder. "Look, I'm glad you told me. You *can* fix this." He grabs another water bottle and hands it to Max. "Pick up extra shifts at the Sanctuary, and we'll cut back your spending. You'll knock this out in no time."

Max exhales deeply. "Thanks, Jamie. I wasn't expecting to word vomit all of this out, but… I actually feel better now."

Jamie laughs. "Just let it all out, Max." He grabs a notebook from the desk and flips it open. "Alright, we're in this together now. Let's think this through." He taps the pen against the page before looking up. "First, we need to see where your money's going. Then… we can figure out where to cut back."

Max nods.

Jamie grins. "Good. Because I want to see you crushing this, not drowning in it."

Max smirks, grabbing a pen from the kitchen table and flipping it smoothly between his fingers, a spark of confidence returning. "Deal. Man, you're the best. I don't know what I'd do without you."

NEXT PAGE.

BUDGETING BASICS

"**O**kay, first things first," Jamie takes a swig of water. "Have you ever thought about where your money goes each month?"

Max rolls his eyes. "I think you know the answer to that by now."

Jamie shakes his head gently. "Don't be too hard on yourself. What you need is a **budget**. Have you seen one before?"

Max looks down, a bit embarrassed. "Not really. Is it like a list or something?"

Jamie smiles. "Sort of! A budget is a plan for how you save and spend your money. It shows what money you have, how much you need to spend on important things like food and bills, and how much you can save. It helps you avoid spending more money than you have."

He clicks his pen. "Let's start with your **income** from Sunday Sanctuary. "How much have you been bringing home each month?"

"About $1,000 when I work overtime," Max says.

"That's good! Now, tell me about your usual **expenses**. What have you been spending money on?"

Max lists his expenses: pizza after work, the occasional day at the pool, and now, his monthly credit card payment.

Jamie looks at Max seriously. "Now comes the important part. Let's sort your expenses into two categories: needs and wants. Needs are things you *have to* spend money on, like your credit card payment. Wants are things you'd *like to* spend money on, but don't absolutely need, like pizza and pool time."

Max nods slowly. "So, the only thing I really *need* to focus on is paying my credit card bill."

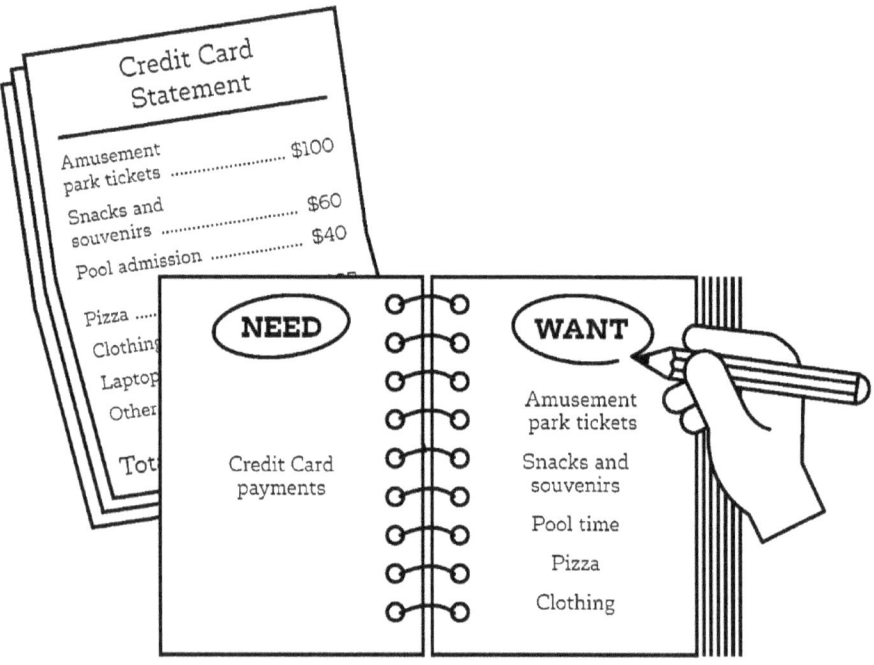

"Exactly," Jamie says. "The credit card payment should be your top priority. The other things can wait until the card is paid off. But don't worry—you don't have to give them up forever. Just for now."

Max thinks back to all the times he chose fun over responsibilities. "I guess my priorities have been all wrong," he says quietly.

Budgeting Basics

Jamie taps his fingers on the notebook. "It happens. But you're taking the right steps now, and that's what matters."

Max exhales, feeling a small flicker of hope beneath his anxiety.

Jamie flips the page and draws a simple chart. "Alright, let's break down how the interest on your credit card works. The card has a 25% **APR**—that's the **annual percentage rate**. Here's what that actually means."

Max watches as Jamie writes down the numbers.

"So, you owe $1,800, and with a 25% APR, your monthly interest is about $37.50. That means next month, if you don't pay back at least that amount, the interest will be added to your balance, and you'll owe even more."

Max's eyes widen. "Wait—so even if I don't spend another dollar, I'll still owe more? That's insane."

Jamie nods and clenches his jaw.

Looking back at the budget, Jamie says, "Since you earn $1,000 a month and don't have any other necessary expenses, you can use most of your paycheck to pay down the credit card. I'd suggest paying $900 toward the bill and saving $100 for emergencies."

"Why not just use all of it?" Max asks.

"You could, but having a small safety net for emergencies is always a good idea. Normally, I'd suggest saving more, but in this case, paying down the card quickly is the better option."

Jamie sketches a simple graph, showing how much of the debt will disappear each month. "At this rate, you'll pay it off in about two months. It's aggressive but think about how free you'll feel when it's done."

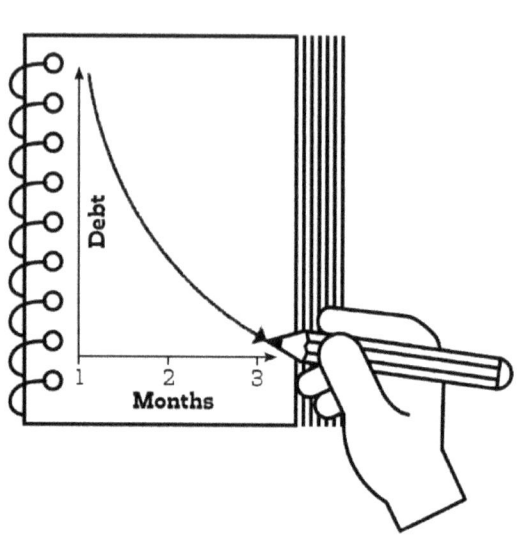

Max studies the plan, a smile tugging at his lips for the first time in a while. "Yeah, I can do this."

"Exactly," Jamie says. "And once it's paid off, you can start saving for other things you need or want, but without the stress."

Max nods. "The timing's actually good. I'll need to start saving for college supplies soon anyway."

Though still a little overwhelmed, Max feels a weight lift from his shoulders. For the first time, he sees a clear path to being debt-free—and it feels doable.

Budgeting Basics

Nice work, you've made it to the end of this journey! What would you like to do next?

- **See what happens if Max doesn't ask Jamie for help. Does he figure it out on his own or spiral further into debt?** HEAD TO THE SILENT STRUGGLE - PAGE 67.

- **Go back and see what happens if Max doesn't choose to buy the laptop right away. Does waiting make a difference?** HEAD TO FINANCIAL FLASHBACK - PAGE 33

Or, if you're ready, head to END OF OUR ADVENTURE - PAGE 75

THE SILENT STRUGGLE

As Max leaves Jamie's house that day, an odd mix of worry and determination swirls inside him. He decides he will tackle his issues alone. It's too embarrassing to share the truth with Jamie. The thrill of using his credit card has long faded, replaced by a nagging sense of dread that he tries to ignore.

Over the next few weeks, Max struggles to keep up his usual cheer as the numbers stack against him. Each time he checks his bank app, the $0 in his savings account feels like a slap in the face.

At night, Max lies awake, replaying the numbers in his head. *How did I let it get this bad?* Sleep doesn't come easily anymore.

He continues to hang out with his friends and order pizza like nothing is wrong, but each card swipe feels heavier than the last. His efforts to manage his money are clumsy, like trying to fix a leaky pipe with tape—it holds for a while, but eventually, the pressure is too much.

One afternoon, Max sits at his desk, his head in his hands. His desk is cluttered with receipts from past outings, and his credit card app is open. The number glaring back at him says: $2,500 owed.

Between hanging out with friends, unplanned spending, and trying to make his credit card payments, there just isn't enough money to go around. His paychecks from Sundae Sanctuary vanish as quickly as they come in.

For the first time, Max doesn't just feel overwhelmed. He feels stuck.

NEXT PAGE.

DENIED AND DISTRAUGHT

The next afternoon, Max and his friends are at their favorite pizza spot. The usual laughter and banter fill the small room as everyone debates what movie to watch later, but Max is mostly silent. When the check arrives, he tosses his credit card onto the pile without thinking.

But when the server returns, his face is apologetic. "Sorry," he says to Max. "Your card was declined."

Max freezes, his cheeks flushing as the words sink in. "What? That can't be right," he stammers, fumbling to grab his phone and check his account. But deep down, he knows exactly what's wrong—he hit his $2,500 limit.

An awkward silence falls over the table. One friend clears their throat, while another suddenly focuses on their phone. "I'll cover you," Jamie offers casually, sliding his card back to the server. Max forces a smile, mumbling, "Thanks. I'll pay you back."

After lunch, Max excuses himself from the group while they head to the movie theater. He replays the moment over and over, the words *"Your card was declined"* ringing in his ears, consumed by the realization that he can't pay for anything anymore.

That night, lying in bed, Max scrolls through his phone, desperately searching for a solution. An ad for a new credit card catches his eye: "Low Interest Rates! Instant Approval!" Hope flickers. *Maybe this can help me out,* he thinks.

Max hurriedly fills out the application, his hands trembling as he types in his information. Moments later, his phone buzzes with an email. He fumbles to open it, his eyes darting across the screen:

"Application Denied."

The words hit him like a punch to the gut. He skims through the rest, his stomach sinking:

Reason for Denial: High credit utilization... low credit score... review your credit report.

Max tosses his phone onto his bed and buries his face in his pillow. He is completely out of options.

The next day, Jamie stops by to drop off a book he borrowed. "Hey, are you okay? And what happened yesterday at lunch?" Jamie asks, sitting down at the kitchen table.

"Oh—that. I'll pay you back soon. Thanks again for covering me," Max manages, looking at the floor.

"I'm not asking for money back. I mean, why did your card get declined?"

Max shifts uncomfortably, and his instinct is to brush off the question. But the weight of his secret feels too heavy to carry any longer. "Jamie... I messed up. Big time."

Jamie leans forward, concern written all over his face. "What's going on?"

Max hesitates for a moment, then spills everything— his inability to manage his money, his maxed-out credit card, the

Denied and Distraught

failed application for a second one, and the overwhelming sense that he's trapped with no way out.

Jamie doesn't miss a beat. "I'm glad you told me. Let's figure this out together."

As they talk, Jamie starts to see how overwhelming the situation really is. It's more than he knows how to handle. So, instead of trying to solve it alone, he helps Max research resources for managing his debt. They find a local financial literacy program, and Max schedules a session with a **financial counselor** named Sophie.

In their first meeting, Sophie greets Max with a kind smile and a clipboard. "Okay, Max, let's break this down," she says, pulling out a chart. "Here's where you are, and here's where we want to go." She points to the current total of his debt and a lower target number.

"We'll tackle this step by step," Sophie explains. "First, we need to minimize your interest payments. Second, we'll create a budget that works for you."

She introduces Max to the concept of categorizing expenses into "needs" and "wants." "*Needs* come first—things like your credit card payments and other essentials. *Wants*, like eating out and entertainment, can wait until we have a better handle on your finances."

Max nods, taking it all in. It feels overwhelming, but Sophie's clear explanations give him a glimmer of hope.

With Sophie's guidance and Jamie's support, Max begins to turn things around. He cuts back on unnecessary spending and puts every spare dollar toward his credit card balance. It's slow going at first, and there are moments when he feels like giving up.

But each month, he notices progress. The balance on his card shrinks, and for the first time in months, he feels like he's regaining control.

As his debt decreases, so does his stress. Max finds himself thinking about his finances in a new way—one focused on planning and **discipline**. He even starts sharing his story with others, hoping to help them avoid the same mistakes.

By the time Max finally pays off his credit card, he feels a sense of accomplishment that goes beyond the numbers. He's learned the hard way how important it is to manage money wisely—and he vows never to let it get out of hand again.

For the first time, Max feels hopeful about his future. And he knows he'll never forget the lessons he learned along the way.

Wow, you've made it to the end of this journey! What would you like to do next?

- **Go back and see what happens if Max asks Jamie for help sooner. How might a single decision change Max's entire path?** HEAD TO CONVERSATIONS AND CHOICES- PAGE 59

Denied and Distraught

- **Go back and see what happens if Max doesn't choose to buy the laptop right away. Does waiting make a difference?** HEAD TO FINANCIAL FLASHBACK- PAGE 33

Or, if you're ready, head to END OF OUR ADVENTURE- PAGE 75

END OF OUR ADVENTURE

What a ride for Max and Jamie! Whether you were walking through the sunny streets of Maplewood, rocking out at a concert, buying a car, or had your credit card application denied, every choice led Jamie and Max—and you—on an adventure through the twists and turns of managing money. Along the way, Max learned the value of budgeting, setting goals, and asking for help when he needed it, and Jamie showed how good habits can make a big difference.

Every financial decision is like a move in a video game—it can influence your (credit) score. Be strategic, and you'll level up in no time! Saving wisely? That's like collecting coins. Sticking to your budget? That's your shield, protecting you from unnecessary expenses. And avoiding debt traps? That's dodging obstacles to stay on course. Even when challenges come your way, remember: every "level" is a chance to learn and grow.

Whether you're saving for a big purchase like a new laptop or simply managing your allowance, try creating a simple budget or starting a savings jar for something fun, like a new game or a movie. Each small step gets you closer to your goals.

And even if things get tough, you're not alone. There's always someone you can turn to for advice—whether it's a family member, a friend, or even a teacher. Remember how Max leaned on Jamie and Sophie to navigate his challenges? You can find your own support team, too.

Hopefully, you had fun exploring these stories and learned a little bit about money along the way. Now it's your turn to apply these lessons in your daily life.

Get ready, set your goals, and start your own adventure! Your financial journey starts now!

TEST YOUR KNOWLEDGE

Coffee, Cereal and Credit

1. How is a credit card like a library card?

2. Jamie explains "interest" to Lily using an example about stickers. Can you explain how interest works with money?

Financial Foundations

1. Mrs. Kelly talks about mindless spending, showing how small purchases can quietly add up. Can you think of any small purchases you've made recently that might seem small on their own, but could add up over time?

2. How could keeping track of these purchases help you manage your money better?

A Walk to Wisdom

1. According to this chapter, how does a credit card work?

2. Lily asks, "Why don't people just use the money they have instead of borrowing it from the bank?" How would you answer Lily's question?

Scoring Points

1. How does Jamie compare building a credit score to playing a video game?
2. What are the potential consequences Jamie mentions if someone doesn't use their credit card responsibly?

Game On!

1. Why does Jamie stop playing the video game, 'Diamond Zone'?
2. What do you think Jamie means when he tells Max that the game is like a "money vacuum?"

Damage Control

1. Max says, "Using a credit card makes it feel like fake money." What does he mean by this?

Diamond Disaster

1. What are the factors that pushed Max to keep playing the video game?

Tech Temptation

1. Why is Jamie hesitant about buying the laptop?
2. How does Jamie use the example of Max's impulse purchase of the drone to try to change his mind about buying the laptop?

Test Your Knowledge

3. Can you think of a time when you bought something on impulse?

Financial Flashback

1. What lesson does Max learn from remembering his uncle's experience with credit card debt, and how does this memory influence his decision about the laptop?
2. Why does Jamie compare Max's uncle's situation to "running in place"?

Scoops and Savings

1. Why does Jamie suggest setting aside money for "emergencies and other things", and how does this idea reflect responsible financial planning?
2. What are other examples of unexpected events that people might need money for?
3. What are the different savings strategies that Max and Jamie propose, and what are the benefits and drawbacks of each approach?

A Cushion for Crisis

1. How do Max's feelings about having an emergency fund change from the beginning of the chapter to the end, and what causes this change?

Concert Conundrum

1. Why does Jamie regret not putting more money into the "other things" fund, and how does this situation illustrate the importance of balancing different financial goals?

Fun and Funds

1. How does the new budgeting plan that Jamie and Max create help them manage their money more effectively?

2. Why is it important to have separate savings for different goals?

Path to Prosperity

1. How did Jamie's and Max's experiences with budgeting and managing their money help them prepare for bigger financial decisions, like buying a car?

2. Why is Jamie's credit score important when buying his first car?

The Impulse Purchase

1. What do you notice about Max's willpower in this chapter?

2. Why does Max end up feeling uneasy after purchasing his dream laptop?

Test Your Knowledge

Debt Dilemma

1. Why is paying only the 'Minimum Due' a bad idea?
2. What are some examples of 'unexpected spending' in this chapter?

Conversations and Choices

1. What does Jamie suggest Max do to pay down his debt?

Budgeting Basics

1. Why does Jamie emphasize the difference between "needs" and "wants" in budgeting?
2. What are some of your "needs" versus "wants"?
3. How might having a high APR (Annual Percentage Rate, or interest rate) on a loan increase your financial burden?

The Silent Struggle

1. What are the risks of trying to handle financial problems alone, and how might asking for help make a difference in Max's situation?

Denied and Distraught

1. How did Max's initial avoidance of his financial problems make his situation worse, and what did he learn from finally seeking help?

2. Why does Max decide to share his story with his peers?

DID YOU KNOW?

1. The average American household carries a credit card debt of over $9,000.
2. Credit card interest rates in the U.S. average around 16% but can go as high as 29% or more.
3. In 2023, American consumers paid over $130 billion in credit card interest and fees.
4. Nearly 70% of Americans have at least one credit card, and the average cardholder has four credit cards.
5. About 40% of American adults carry credit card debt from month to month.
6. Missing a credit card payment can result in late fees ranging from $25 to $40 and can also increase your interest rate.
7. Consistently carrying high credit card balances can negatively impact your credit score, making it harder to get loans or new credit.
8. Many credit cards offer rewards and cash back, but the interest on unpaid balances can quickly outweigh these benefits.
9. Over 80 million Americans applied for new credit cards in 2023.
10. On average, it takes about 12 years to pay off a credit card debt of $5,000 if you only make the minimum payment each month.

11. High levels of credit card debt can lead to financial stress, affecting mental and physical health.
12. A significant number of Americans don't know their credit card's interest rate, which can lead to unexpected financial strain.
13. Young adults between the ages of 18 and 24 are more likely to max out their credit cards than any other age group.
14. Credit card companies can change your interest rate if you miss a payment, making it even harder to pay off your debt.
15. Many Americans use credit cards to cover emergency expenses, highlighting the importance of having an emergency savings fund.

GLOSSARY

Allowance: Money given to you regularly, often by parents, to spend or save as you choose. It's a good way to learn about managing money. While this word isn't used in the book, Jamie and Max might get a weekly allowance to save for a new game or spend at the arcade.

Annual Percentage Rate (APR): The yearly rate that represents the total cost of borrowing money on your credit card or loan, expressed as a percentage. In the book, this is also referred to as Max's credit card interest rate. For example, Max learns how his credit card debt grows because of the high APR.

Balance: The amount of money you have in your bank account, or the amount you owe on a credit card or loan. Jamie checks his savings account balance to see how much he can spend or save for his goals, like buying a laptop. Max checks his credit card balance to track how much he owes the bank.

Bank: A place where you keep your money safe, borrow money, or get other financial services.

Budget: A plan that shows how much money you expect to receive and how you will spend it. Jamie and Max create a budget to manage their money better, making sure they can save for things like a laptop, emergencies, and school supplies. Jamie also helps Max create a budget to pay his debt back more quickly.

Budgeting: The act of creating a budget. This helps you keep track of your money so you don't spend more than you have. Jamie helps Max learn budgeting to get his spending under control.

Credit Card: A card issued by a bank that lets you borrow money to buy things. You need to pay back the money later. Jamie wants to get a credit card to learn how to manage money and build a good credit score.

Credit Card Bill: A monthly statement from the bank that shows what you've bought with your credit card, how much you owe, and when you need to pay it back.

Credit Check & **Credit Report**: A credit report is a detailed record of your credit history, showing how well you manage money—like whether you pay your bills on time and how much debt you have. A credit check happens when a lender, such as a bank or car dealership, reviews your credit report to decide how much money they can lend you and what interest rate to charge.

Credit Limit: The maximum amount of money you're allowed to borrow on a credit card. Once you hit that limit, you can't borrow more until you pay some back.

Credit Score: A number that tells lenders how good you are at paying back money. A high score shows you are reliable and may get better interest rates for loans. Jamie builds a good credit score by paying off his credit card in full and avoiding carrying a balance.

Glossary

Debt: Money that you owe to someone else. Max gets into debt with the bank when he spends too much on his credit card without being able to pay it off right away.

Down Payment: When you buy a car, you don't have to pay the full price upfront. Instead, you pay part of the cost right away—that's the down payment. It shows you're serious about the purchase and reduces the amount you need to borrow. If you stop making your payments and the lender takes the car back, you don't get your down payment back.

Expenses: The money you spend on things you need or want. Max struggles with his expenses when he spends too much on summer activities.

Finance (verb): To buy something with credit, usually by taking a loan that you pay back over time with interest. For example, Jamie finances a car, borrowing money from the car dealership and agreeing to make regular payments with interest.

Finances: Your money and how you manage it, including savings, expenses, and debts. Jamie and Max learn to manage their finances to avoid problems like debt.

Financial Counselor: A person who helps you understand how to manage your money better. When Max feels overwhelmed by his credit card debt, he talks to a financial counselor, who helps him create a plan to pay it back.

Fund: A sum of money saved for a particular purpose. Max and Jamie create a "laptop fund" to save money specifically for buying new laptops.

Impulse Spending: Buying things suddenly without planning or thinking about whether you need them or can afford them. For example, Max buys an expensive laptop on a whim, which makes it harder for him to manage his money.

Income: Money that you earn from a job. Max and Jamie earn income from their jobs at the ice cream shop to pay for expenses and save for future needs.

Interest: The cost of borrowing money, which you pay as a fee along with the amount you borrowed. You calculate the interest you owe using the interest rate. Max learns how a high interest rate (or APR) makes it harder to pay off his credit card debt.

Interest Rate: The percentage of extra money you pay when you borrow money. It is also referred to as the Annual Percentage Rate, or APR. A higher rate means you pay back more.

Loan: Money you borrow from a bank, car dealership, or another person that you must pay back with interest. Jamie takes out a loan to help pay for his car.

Minimum Due: The smallest amount you can pay on your credit card bill to avoid penalties. Max learns that only paying the minimum due leads to more debt over time.

Prioritize: To decide what is most important and focus on that first. For example, Max prioritizes paying off his credit card debt before saving for emergencies.

Glossary

Savings: Money you put aside to use later, often for something special like a new bike or a trip. Jamie and Max save part of their income from the ice cream shop to buy a new laptop, showing the importance of saving for big purchases.

Savings Account: A special bank account where you keep your money safe. The bank might add extra money, called interest, to help your savings grow over time.

Self-Discipline: The ability to control yourself and make good choices even when it's hard. Max develops self-discipline to stop using his credit card impulsively, helping him manage his finances better.

NOTES

Notes

Notes

www.ingramcontent.com/pod-product-compliance
Lightning Source LLC
Chambersburg PA
CBHW070644030426
42337CB00020B/4154